CHARLES SCHNIEIDER

Charting the Seas of Indie Development

Helpful Tips and Mistakes to Avoid on Making Your First Game as an Aspiring Indie developer

This book was professionally typeset on Reedsy.
Find out more at reedsy.com

Contents

1 Introduction - Sailing the Uncharted Seas   1
2 Getting Started- Setting Sail on the Creative Horizon   3
3 The Calm Before the Storm - Navigating the Pre-
   Development...   6
4 Forging the Foundations - Navigating the Development Seas   9
5 Painting the Canvas - Artistry and Design Amidst the...   12
6 The Art of Coding - Navigating the Digital Reefs
   and Shoals   15
7 Navigating Monetization Strategies - Sailing the Commerce... 18
8 Navigating the Seas of Marketing and Promotion
   - Hoisting...   21
9 Anchoring in the Community - Navigating the
   Waters of...   24
10 Navigating the Launch and Beyond - Setting Sail
   for Glory   27
11 Charting the Waters of Wisdom - Navigating the
   Realm of...   30
12 A Reflection on the Indie Odyssey- The Harbor's Embrace   33
13 References   36

1

Introduction - Sailing the Uncharted Seas

An Overview of the indie game development landscape

Set sail, all you aspiring game developers, into the vast ocean of indie game creation where unexplored islands of creativity await discovery. The indie game development landscape, much like the open sea, is a realm where untold stories lie beneath the surface, waiting for intrepid souls to bring them ashore. Charting a course into this uncharted territory is an adventure in itself, with dangers and treasures aplenty.

The Importance of guidance for new developers

In the tumultuous seas of indie game development, guidance is your compass, guiding you through the storms and steering you away from the perilous reefs that threaten to wreck your dreams. A mentor is like an experienced navigator, sharing the tales of their own voyages, offering wisdom gained from weathering the unpredictable tides. As we embark on this chapter, understand that the journey is not a solo expedition; it's a crewed vessel, and the guidance of seasoned sailors can make all the difference.

A Brief outline of the Journey Ahead

Our odyssey into the uncharted seas of indie game development is a daring escapade, akin to a pirate's quest for buried treasure. We begin by unraveling the cartography of game design, where every line of code is a plotted course, and every pixel on the screen is a marker on our nautical map. Navigating the vast expanse, we navigate the intricate passages of character design, breathing life into the digital crew that will populate our virtual galleons.

As we set sail, the challenges grow more formidable — tackling the tempestuous waters of gameplay mechanics and the intricate dance of storytelling on the high seas. Yet with each revelation, we gain the tools to navigate through the hidden coves of indie game development. As we navigate these waters, let the knowledge bestowed upon us be the wind in our sails, propelling us forward through the murky depths of the uncharted seas. May our creative spirits guide us, like the North Star in the night sky, through the shadows that dance on the horizon of the distant skies of your first indie project..

2

Getting Started- Setting Sail on the Creative Horizon

Finding Inspiration

Exploring Diverse Sources

Like the morning sun kisses the waves, casting a golden glow upon the vast expanse of the creative horizon, our journey begins with the quest for inspiration. Much like seasoned sailors combing uncharted shores for hidden treasures, indie game developers must cast a wide net across diverse sources. Dive into the ocean of literature, traverse the landscapes of art, and wander through the bustling ports of everyday life. From the whispers of the wind to the tales spun by fellow sailors, inspiration lies hidden in the most unexpected of places.

The wise mariner knows that innovation thrives in the open sea of ideas. Venture beyond the familiar islands and explore the uncharted territories, for it is in the unknown that the seeds of groundbreaking concepts await discovery. Whether it be the ethereal glow of biolumi-nescent creatures beneath the ocean's surface or the rhythmic cadence of a bustling market square, draw inspiration from the mosaic of life that surrounds us.

Identifying Personal Passions

As sailors connect with the sea, so must game developers connect with their innermost passions. The heart of every great game beats with the rhythm of the creator's fervor. Identify the elements that ignite the flames of your own creative spirit. Is it the allure of ancient myths or the intrigue of futuristic realms? Uncover the buried treasures within your own soul, for it is these personal passions that will infuse your game with authenticity and captivate the hearts of those who embark on this virtual voyage with you.

Setting Clear Goals

Defining the Purpose of the Game

With the compass in hand and the sails billowing with the winds of inspiration, it is time to chart the course with a clear sense of purpose. Define the very essence of your game – what story does it yearn to tell, and what emotions does it seek to evoke? Is it a swashbuckling adventure, a mystery shrouded in shadows, or perhaps a tale of love that transcends time? The purpose is the North Star that guides every decision and action, ensuring a cohesive journey through the creative seas.

Establishing Realistic Milestones

Just as a seasoned captain maps out the journey with waypoints, indie game developers must establish realistic milestones. The sea may be vast, but breaking down the expedition into manageable tasks ensures progress amid the ebb and flow of the creative process. From coding challenges to design intricacies, each milestone is a port of call, a place to restock supplies, and a chance to reflect on the journey thus far.

In this creative odyssey, setting sail without clear goals is akin to navigating through a fog-shrouded sea without a compass. Embrace the spirit of adventure but anchor your aspirations in the concrete reality of achievable milestones. By doing so, you equip yourself to weather the storms and bask in the glory of reaching each plotted destination on the expansive map of your game development voyage.

3

The Calm Before the Storm - Navigating the Pre-Development Waters

Market Research

Analyzing the Target Audience

As the horizon stretches before us, it's time to cast the spyglass upon the vast sea of potential players. Market research becomes the navigator's compass, guiding us toward the understanding of the target audience. Just as the stars illuminate the night sky, delve into demographics, preferences, and player behaviors. Who are the seekers of our virtual treasures? What winds of entertainment sway their sails? Analyze, adapt, and align your course with the currents of player desires, for a game that resonates with its audience becomes a beacon in the crowded seas of indie game development.

Studying Successful Indie Games

The seasoned sailor learns from the tales of those who have navigated these waters before. Study the charts of successful indie games, exploring the nuances that propelled them to greatness. What winds caught their sails, and what hidden reefs did they avoid? Assemble your own atlas of inspiration, drawing upon the successes and failures of those who have sailed the indie seas. The currents of innovation often flow from the tributaries of lessons learned, and by studying the achievements of others, you fortify your vessel against the storms of uncertainty.

Planning and Documentation

Creating a Comprehensive Game Design Document

With the map of the market in hand, it's time to chart the specifics of our own voyage. The game design document becomes our navigational chart, outlining the contours of the virtual landscapes we aim to explore. Detail the lore that breathes life into the game, sketch the characters that will inhabit these digital realms, and articulate the mechanics that will propel players through the interactive tides. A comprehensive game design document is the sextant that ensures precision in execution, offering a roadmap for both the captain and the crew.

Outlining the Development Timeline

As the stars move across the celestial canvas, time becomes a precious commodity. Outlining the development timeline is akin to plotting the course of the celestial bodies. Break down the journey into manageable phases, assigning each milestone a date on the cosmic calendar. From the first stroke of the code to the final polish, the development timeline ensures that the winds of creativity are harnessed efficiently. Like the steady rhythm of the ship's heartbeat, adhere to the outlined plan, adjusting sails as needed but always keeping the destination in sight.

In the pre-development phase, as we anchor in the calm waters before the storm, let the knowledge gained from market research and meticulous planning be the ballast that steadies our vessel. The storm may rage, but with a well-prepared crew and a detailed map, we navigate through the seas of uncertainty with confidence. As we prepare to set sail into the tumultuous waters of development, our charts and compasses shall guide us through the unpredictable waves that await on the next leg of our indie odyssey.

4

Forging the Foundations - Navigating the Development Seas

Choosing the Right Tools

Selecting Game Engines and Development Platforms

As our vessel embarks on the turbulent seas of development, the choice of tools becomes the captain's decree. Just as a skilled sailor selects the right ship for the journey, so must we carefully choose game engines and development platforms. Unity, with its versatile winds, or the robust stability of Unreal Engine — the decision shapes the very essence of our voyage. Navigate the market winds, consider the waters your vessel is set to traverse, and choose tools that align with the vision of the game you aim to craft.

Explore the archipelago of development platforms, from PC to console to mobile, and weigh the anchors of compatibility. The right tools are the sails that catch the gusts of creativity, propelling your game forward. Seek counsel from fellow sailors who have sailed these digital waters, and let the collective wisdom guide your hand as you hoist the colors of your chosen tools.

Exploring Essential Software and Resources

In the expansive sea of development, every sailor needs a toolkit. Navigate through the digital marketplaces and harbor essential software and resources. From graphic design tools like Adobe Creative Cloud to version control systems like Git, equip your crew with the instruments needed to forge the intricate elements of your game. Dive into the treasure troves of online communities and forums, where fellow developers share maps to uncharted territories and unveil the secrets of successful navigation.

Prototyping and Iteration

Building a Basic Prototype

As the shipwright lays the keel, so must the game developer construct the basic prototype. The prototype is the ship in its infancy, a vessel to test the waters and ensure that the design aligns with the intended vision. Sail into the uncharted coves of gameplay mechanics, unfurl the canvas of user interface design, and let the prototype be the first ripple in the vast ocean of your game's potential.

Embracing Feedback and Iteration

The waves of feedback crash upon the shores of progress, sculpting the game into its final form. Embrace the gusts of critique, for they are the zephyrs that guide your vessel toward perfection. Sailors of old revised their maps with every discovery, and so must you iterate upon your game. From player feedback to the insights of your development crew, let the iterative process be the wind in your sails, propelling your creation toward excellence.

In the development essentials phase, the ship of your game takes form on the open seas of creation. As you choose your tools and navigate through the trials of prototyping, remember that the storms of development are weathered with resilience and flexibility. The tools are your compass, the prototype your first voyage, and the iterations are the continual adjustments to steer your vessel toward the greatness that awaits on the horizon of completion.

5

Painting the Canvas - Artistry and Design Amidst the Creative Storm

Creating a Visual Identity

Establishing a Consistent Art Style

As our vessel cuts through the digital waves, the visual identity becomes the flag that flutters atop the mast, declaring our game's presence to the world. Just as a ship's figurehead embodies its spirit, establish a consistent art style that breathes life into your creation. Will your game be adorned with the vibrant hues of a painter's palette, or will it tread the shadows of a noir landscape? Navigate the waters of artistic expression, anchoring your vision in a style that resonates with the essence of your game.

Craft the visual identity with purpose, for it is the first impression cast upon the eyes of the player. From character design to environmental aesthetics, each stroke of the virtual brush contributes to the tapestry of your game. Sail through the vast inspirations of art history, from the sweeping landscapes of Romanticism to the avant-garde expressions of modernism, and weave a visual narrative that echoes the heartbeat of your creation.

Crafting Memorable Characters and Environments

In the expansive seas of game development, characters and environments are the islands that beckon players to explore. Craft characters with depth, each with a story etched in their virtual veins. The protagonist is the captain of the ship, and the supporting cast are the crew that adds flavor to the journey. Environments, like uncharted territories, should be both awe-inspiring and immersive. From the bustling ports to the serene horizons, each pixel contributes to the world-building that transforms your game into a living, breathing entity.

User Interface Design

Prioritizing User Experience

As we navigate through the visuals, the compass of user interface design guides players through the interactive waters. Prioritize user experience, ensuring that every element enhances rather than hinders the journey. The user interface is the sextant of player interaction, allowing them to navigate through the complexities of your creation. Strive for intuitive design, where the helm of interaction feels like second nature to the player.

Testing and Refining Interface Elements

Just as a ship undergoes sea trials before its maiden voyage, the user interface must be tested and refined. Sail through the turbulent waters of usability testing, gathering feedback to refine the elements that may disrupt the flow of the player's experience. Iteration in the design phase is the polishing of the ship's hull, ensuring that every aspect of the user interface aligns with the overall aesthetic and functionality.

In the artistry and design phase, the canvas of your game becomes a masterpiece in the making. As you shape the visual identity and design the user interface, remember that every stroke of creativity contributes to the immersive experience awaiting players. The storm of creation may rage, but with a well-crafted vessel adorned with captivating visuals and intuitive design, your game sails confidently toward the horizon of player engagement.

6

The Art of Coding - Navigating the Digital Reefs and Shoals

Code Organization

Embracing Modular Programming

As our digital vessel sails through the complex waters of programming, the art of code organization becomes the captain's log, chronicling the journey of creation. Embrace modular programming, for just as a ship's compartments house different functions, well-organized code structures compartmentalize functionalities within your game. Each module, like a well-stocked hold, contains the intricacies of specific features, allowing for easier maintenance and troubleshooting.

Navigate through the intricate architecture of your codebase, building a framework where each module interacts seamlessly. The modularity of code is the wind in the sails of collaboration, enabling multiple developers to work on different components concurrently. Like a well-orchestrated symphony, modular programming harmonizes the diverse elements of your game, ensuring that each piece contributes to the overall composition.

Documenting Code for Collaboration

In the vast sea of collaborative development, documentation becomes the navigational charts that guide sailors through the intricacies of your code. Document with purpose, leaving behind a trail of knowledge for fellow developers who may join the crew. Just as a ship's log records the winds and currents, your code documentation should detail the logic and purpose behind each line. A well-documented codebase is the treasure map that leads developers to the heart of your creation, unraveling the mysteries and fostering a culture of shared understanding.

Performance Optimization

Implementing Efficient Coding Practices

As our digital vessel faces the tempest of performance demands, efficient coding practices become the sturdy sails that harness the winds of optimization. Write code with efficiency in mind, optimizing algorithms and data structures to ensure that the game sails smoothly on a sea of computational resources. Like a captain calculating the most favorable course, make informed decisions on memory usage, processing power, and network bandwidth to steer your game toward peak performance.

Testing and Optimizing Game Performance

In the ever-shifting tides of game development, testing is the compass that guides you toward performance optimization. Conduct rigorous testing across different devices, platforms, and scenarios to uncover bottlenecks and inefficiencies. Just as a ship undergoes stress tests, subject your game to the trials of real-world usage. Optimize the code based on performance metrics, ensuring that your creation not only weathers the storm of player engagement but does so with finesse and speed.

In the art of coding, the symphony of organization and optimization creates a harmonious composition that propels your game to new heights. As you embrace modular programming and document for collaboration, remember that the true beauty lies not just in functionality but in the clarity of understanding for those who navigate the code you have created.

7

Navigating Monetization Strategies - Sailing the Commerce Waters

Exploring Business Models

Choosing Between Free-to-Play and Premium

As our digital vessel sails into the commercial waters, the choice of business model becomes the navigator's compass, directing the course of monetary tides. Choose between the two cardinal directions of free-to-play and premium, each carrying its own set of opportunities and challenges. The free-to-play model casts a wide net, enticing players aboard without an upfront cost, relying on in-app purchases and ads to sustain the voyage. On the other hand, the premium model demands an upfront fee for the ticket to adventure, promising an immersive experience without the interruption of in-game advertisements.

Navigate through the market currents, studying successful games that have navigated these monetization waters. Consider the player demographics, the nature of your game, and the expectations of the virtual travelers you aim to attract. The business model is the anchor that secures your vessel's place in the bustling harbors of digital commerce.

Incorporating In-App Purchases and Ads

In the sea of potential revenue streams, in-app purchases and advertisements become the cargo that sustains the ship. For free-to-play games, in-app purchases are the treasures sought by players willing to enhance their journey with virtual goods, upgrades, or cosmetic enhancements. Ads, like passing ships paying tolls, contribute to the coffers as players engage with promotional content.

Carefully implement these revenue mechanisms, ensuring they enhance rather than detract from the player experience. In-app purchases should feel like a visit to a bustling marketplace, offering value and delight. Ads should be the gentle breeze, subtly enriching the player's journey without capsizing the vessel with intrusiveness.

Pricing and Marketing

Setting a Competitive Price

In the marketplace where myriad vessels compete for attention, setting a competitive price is the sail that catches the winds of player interest. For premium games, establish a price that reflects the value of the experience you offer. Study the market, analyze the pricing of comparable games, and position your creation as a worthy investment for virtual adventurers.

Planning Effective Marketing Strategies

As the ship sails into the horizon, the call of the market beckons for effective marketing strategies. Chart a course through the marketing seas, utilizing social media, influencers, and traditional channels to spread the word. Craft a narrative that captivates potential players, showcasing the unique features and experiences that set your game apart. The marketing strategy is the sextant that guides players toward the shores of discovery, enticing them to embark on the virtual journey you've meticulously crafted.

In the commerce waters, where the tides of revenue ebb and flow, the choice of business model, incorporation of revenue streams, and effective pricing and marketing become the helm that steers your game toward success. As we prepare to embark on the final leg of our indie odyssey, let the lessons learned in monetization strategies be the wind that fills the sails, propelling your vessel toward the horizon of commercial triumph.

8

Navigating the Seas of Marketing and Promotion - Hoisting the Colors

Building an Online Presence

Leveraging Social Media

As our digital vessel sets sail upon the vast sea of potential players, building an online presence becomes the wind that carries whispers of our creation to every corner of the gaming world. Social media, the bustling ports of the digital age, offers a platform to broadcast the tales of our indie odyssey. Harness the power of Twitter, Facebook, Instagram, and other social networks to connect with fellow sailors and potential passengers alike. Share glimpses of the development journey, from concept art teasers to behind-the-scenes anecdotes, creating a community that eagerly awaits the unveiling of your creation.

Engage with the virtual populace, respond to their comments and questions, and let the waves of anticipation swell. Social media is not just a tool but a living, breathing ecosystem where the echoes of your game can become a chorus that reverberates across the gaming seas.

Establishing a Developer Website

In the age of digital exploration, a developer website becomes the lighthouse that guides interested voyagers to your creation. Establish a central hub where curious players can anchor and explore the lore, features, and development progress of your game. Design the website like a well-charted map, intuitive and informative, providing a seamless navigation experience for those who seek to learn more.

The developer website is not merely a showcase but a dynamic port where players can sign up for newsletters, engage in forums, and download demos or beta versions. Let the website be the anchor that keeps players tethered to your journey, eagerly awaiting the day they can set sail on the digital seas you've crafted.

Crafting a Compelling Trailer

Showcasing Key Features

As our vessel gains visibility on the horizon, crafting a compelling trailer becomes the signal fires that draw the attention of sailors near and far. The trailer is the anthem of your creation, a visual and auditory masterpiece that resonates with the very soul of your game. Showcase the key features that make your creation unique — the captivating landscapes, the engaging gameplay mechanics, and the characters that breathe life into the digital realm.

The trailer is a journey in itself, narrated by the music, paced by the visuals, and guided by the voice that speaks the language of excitement and anticipation. Make every second count, offering a glimpse of the wonders that await players as they embark on the voyage of your game.

Creating Engaging Promotional Materials

As the sails billow with the winds of promotion, create engaging materials that become the scrolls and maps carried by messengers across the gaming world. Design eye-catching posters, captivating banners, and alluring social media graphics. Let the promotional materials be the heralds that proclaim the arrival of a gaming experience worth exploring.

Craft a visual identity that is consistent across all materials, reinforcing the brand and creating a cohesive narrative. From teaser images to countdowns, every piece of promotional material should echo the excitement that emanates from the heart of your creation.

In the seas of marketing and promotion, where visibility is the wind that fills the sails of player interest, the building of an online presence, crafting a compelling trailer, and creating engaging promotional materials become the navigation tools that guide your game toward the bustling harbors of player engagement. As sail ever closer to the final chapter of our indie odyssey, may the marketing strategies be the beacon that guides your vessel to a triumphant arrival on the shores of player acclaim.

9

Anchoring in the Community - Navigating the Waters of Engagement

Connecting with the Audience

Responding to Player Feedback

As our digital vessel sails through the seas of development, connecting with the audience becomes the camaraderie that forges a bond between creators and players. Listen to the echoes of player feedback, for they are the winds that carry whispers of improvement and innovation. Respond to comments, engage in discussions, and let the players feel the pulse of their influence on the journey.

A responsive development crew is akin to a ship's crew that adjusts the sails based on the changing winds. Implement player suggestions where possible, address concerns promptly, and showcase the collaborative spirit that shapes the game's voyage. The audience is not merely spectators; they are fellow sailors, contributing to the narrative of your creation.

Building a Community Around the Game

In the vast archipelago of gaming, building a community around your creation becomes the vibrant port where players congregate. Create forums, Discord servers, and social media groups where players can share their experiences, insights, and fan theories. Foster an environment where the community becomes an extension of the game itself, weaving stories and friendships that transcend the digital realm.

Engage with the community through regular updates, exclusive behind-the-scenes content, and interactive events. The community is not just an audience; they are the crew that breathes life into the sails of your game, propelling it forward with enthusiasm and camaraderie.

Early Access and Beta Testing

Leveraging Player Insights

As the ship nears completion, early access and beta testing become the sea trials where the vessel is put to the test by eager adventurers. Leverage the insights of players who embark on this early voyage, for they are the navigators who chart the course through uncharted territories. Early access allows players to experience the game in its evolving state, providing invaluable feedback on mechanics, balancing, and overall experience.

Beta testing is not just a phase but a collaborative endeavor, a union of developers and players striving toward a common goal. Dive deep into player insights, adjust the sails based on their experiences, and let the beta testing phase be the refining fire that prepares your vessel for the grand launch.

Building Anticipation for the Full Release

In the final stretch before the full release, build anticipation among the community like the rising tide that lifts the ship. Showcase the improvements made based on player feedback, unveil teasers of what's to come, and stoke the flames of excitement. Leverage the community's enthusiasm to create a crescendo of anticipation that echoes through the gaming world.

Offer exclusive sneak peeks, countdowns, and interactive events that involve the community in the final preparations. The full release is not just the end of the journey; it's a celebration shared with the community that has been there through every wave and storm.

In the seas of community engagement, where players are not just spectators but active participants, connecting with the audience and navigating through early access and beta testing become the compass that guides your game toward a successful launch. As we prepare to unfurl the final sails and set course for the grand release, may the community engagement strategies be the anchor that steadies your vessel in the midst of excitement and anticipation.

10

Navigating the Launch and Beyond - Setting Sail for Glory

Launch Planning

Creating a Launch Strategy

As our vessel nears the grand launch, creating a launch strategy becomes the navigation chart that ensures a triumphant entry into the gaming seas. Plot the course meticulously, considering the timing, platform releases, and marketing efforts that will propel your creation into the spotlight. Design a launch event that echoes like a cannon shot across the gaming world, capturing the attention of players far and wide.

Utilize the community built over the development journey, engaging them as ambassadors to spread the word. Leverage social media, gaming influencers, and press coverage to amplify the message. The launch strategy is not just about the release; it's a celebration that marks the culmination of years of hard work and dedication.

Ensuring a Polished and Bug-Free Release

As the ship embarks on its maiden voyage, ensuring a polished and bug-free release becomes the meticulous preparation that guarantees a smooth sail. Conduct thorough testing, addressing any issues or bugs that may mar the player experience. Just as a captain inspects the ship before setting sail, test the waters across different devices, platforms, and scenarios to ensure a seamless launch.

A polished release is the flag hoisted high, signaling to players that your vessel is not just a creation but a finely crafted experience. Be vigilant during the launch, ready to address any unforeseen challenges that may arise. A smooth launch is not just a moment; it's the prologue to the immersive journey that awaits players.

Post-Launch Support

Providing Regular Updates

As the ship navigates the waters of post-launch, providing regular updates becomes the steady breeze that keeps the sails full. Continue the journey beyond the release date, offering players new content, features, and improvements. Just as a ship evolves with each port of call, let your game grow with each update, expanding the horizons of player experience.

Communicate transparently with the community, sharing the roadmap of upcoming updates and soliciting their input. Regular updates are not just patches but chapters in an ongoing saga, keeping players engaged and excited for the continued voyage.

Addressing Player Feedback and Issues

In the wake of launch, addressing player feedback and issues becomes the attentive navigation that ensures your vessel stays on course. Listen to the echoes of the community, acknowledging their triumphs and concerns alike. Engage in open communication through forums, social media, and developer blogs, letting players know that their voices are heard and valued.

Swiftly address any issues that arise, releasing patches and hotfixes to keep the ship sailing smoothly. The post-launch phase is not just about maintenance but about fostering a relationship with the community that extends beyond the initial excitement of release.

In the waters of launch and post-launch, where the success of the voyage is measured by player satisfaction and continued engagement, creating a launch strategy and ensuring a polished release are the flags that herald the arrival. As we navigate the ongoing journey of updates and player interaction, may the post-launch strategies be the compass that guides your vessel toward the enduring glory that comes with a well-supported and beloved game.

11

Charting the Waters of Wisdom - Navigating the Realm of Learning and Growth

Reflecting on the Development Journey

Analyzing Successes and Challenges

As our vessel sails into the calmer waters of reflection, analyzing the successes and challenges of the development journey becomes the logbook that documents the lessons etched in the sails of experience. Take stock of the triumphs that propelled your creation to new heights, and scrutinize the challenges that tested the resilience of your crew. What currents led to smooth sailing, and what storms brought unforeseen tempests?

Reflect on player feedback, market reception, and the impact of your marketing and development strategies. Just as a captain reviews the ship's course after each voyage, analyze the course of your development journey. Celebrate the victories, learn from the setbacks, and let the reflections shape the course for future endeavors.

Extracting Lessons for Future Projects

In the stillness of introspection, extract the pearls of wisdom that lie beneath the surface of the development journey. What methodologies proved effective, and which proved treacherous waters? Were there moments where innovation flourished, or instances where familiar shores brought unexpected challenges?

The lessons extracted are the guiding stars for future projects. Consider how collaboration, marketing strategies, and development processes can be refined. The experiences of the past are not just waypoints; they are beacons illuminating the path toward greater mastery in the ever-evolving landscape of game development.

Continuous Learning

Staying Informed About Industry Trends

As our vessel anchors in the harbor of continuous learning, staying informed about industry trends becomes the compass that points toward the cutting edge. The gaming industry, like the sea, is ever-changing, with new currents and winds shaping the landscape. Dive into industry publications, attend conferences, and engage with the developer community to stay abreast of the latest trends, technologies, and player preferences.

Just as a skilled navigator reads the stars to anticipate changes in weather, stay attuned to the industry's shifts. This knowledge is not just about staying relevant; it's about positioning your vessel to ride the crest of innovation in future endeavors.

Exploring New Technologies and Techniques

In the uncharted waters of tomorrow's development, exploring new technologies and techniques becomes the telescope that reveals distant horizons. Embrace emerging technologies, from virtual and augmented reality to advancements in artificial intelligence. Experiment with new development methodologies, tools, and design principles that may redefine the very nature of your creations.

The willingness to explore is the spirit of discovery that has fueled the evolution of gaming. Just as ancient mariners sailed beyond the known seas, explore new territories of creativity and technology. The journey of learning is not a destination; it's an endless horizon that expands with each wave of innovation.

In the realm of learning and growth, where the voyage is not confined to a single creation but extends into the boundless potential of future projects, reflecting on the development journey and continuous learning become the sextant and compass that guide your vessel toward ever-greater mastery. As we prepare to dock in the harbor of this indie odyssey, may the lessons learned and the knowledge gained become the treasures that enrich the journey onward.

12

A Reflection on the Indie Odyssey- The Harbor's Embrace

Conclusion

Recap of Key Tips and Takeaways

As our indie odyssey nears its conclusion, let us cast a final gaze upon the navigational charts and whispered winds that have guided our vessel through the expansive seas of game development. A recap of key tips and takeaways serves as the compass rose that summarizes the wisdom gained:

- **Setting Sail with Purpose**: From the inception of an idea to the launch of a game, purpose guides every stroke of creativity. Define the vision, establish clear goals, and let purpose be the lodestar that illuminates the path.
- **Community as Crew**: The community is not just an audience; they are fellow sailors on this journey. Build connections, engage with players, and let the community be the wind that fills the sails

of your game.

- **Iterative Course Correction:** Just as a ship adjusts its course in response to changing winds, iterate on your game. Embrace player feedback, address issues promptly, and let the journey be a continuous evolution toward excellence.
- **Adaptability in Storms:** Storms may rise unexpectedly. Be adaptable, adjust sails, and weather the challenges with resilience. In the unpredictability of game development, adaptability is the sturdy hull that sees your vessel through tumultuous waters.
- **Learning from Every Wave:** Reflect on successes and challenges alike. Extract lessons, for every wave in the development journey carries wisdom. Learning is not just a destination; it's a perpetual voyage toward mastery.

Encouragement for the Indie Developer's Journey

As we approach the harbor's embrace, let these final words be the anchor that steadies your vessel:

The indie developer's journey is not merely about creating games; it's a testament to creativity, perseverance, and the unyielding spirit of exploration. The seas may be vast, and the challenges may seem insurmountable, but remember, each wave you navigate, each storm you weather, is a testament to your passion and dedication.

In the harbor, take a moment to savor the journey—the highs of creativity, the camaraderie of the community, and the lessons learned in the challenges faced. The harbor is not just an end; it's a juncture where you replenish supplies, celebrate triumphs, and prepare for the next leg of your voyage.

As the captain of your creation, may you continue to navigate the seas of game development with unwavering determination. The indie odyssey is not a solitary venture; it's a shared narrative with players, fellow developers, and the ever-evolving landscape of the industry.

Take pride in the vessel you've crafted, the stories you've woven, and the impact you've made on the gaming world. The harbor awaits, but the seas of possibility stretch beyond. As you set sail into future endeavors, may your creativity be boundless, your sails ever-filled, and your indie odyssey a perpetual voyage toward new horizons.

Fair winds, fellow sailor, and may your creations continue to chart courses in the hearts of players for generations to come.

13

References

ChatGPT: OpenAI (2021). ChatGPT (GPT-4) (Software) OpenAI. https//www.openai.com